POLISH YOUR SOUL
AND SPRUCE UP YOUR HEART:

How to like what you see in the mirror

By Anne Bryan Smollin, CSJ, PhD

Author of "Jiggle Your Heart
and Tickle Your Soul"

For information about ordering more copies of this book, write:

Counseling for Laity
40 North Main Ave.
Albany, New York 12203

First Printing, November 1996
Second Printing, April 1997

Cover design by James Breig and
Donna Wait Lesson

Publisher: Canticle Press
             371 Watervliet-Shaker Rd.
             Latham, NY 12110-4741
Library of Congress Catalog Card
Number: 96-092886
ISBN: 0-9641725-3-4

DEDICATION

To those of you who have been blessings
in my life —
who share joy and laughter with me —
who are always there for me —
....you give me life

especially to my Mom and sister Kay
and my CSJ community

FUN READINGS

Borysenko, Joan. POCKETFUL OF MIRACLES, New York: Warner Books, Inc., 1994

Goodheart, Annette. LAUGHTER THERAPY. Santa Barbara: Less Stress Press, 1994.

Goodman, Joel. LAFFIRMATIONS. Florida: Health Communications, Inc., 1995.

Klein, Allen. THE HEALING POWER OF HUMOR. Los Angeles: Jeremy P. Tarcher, Inc. 1989.

Moody, Raymond A., Jr. LAUGH AFTER LAUGH. Jacksonville, Florida: Headwaters Press, 1978.

Paulson, Terry L. MAKING HUMOR WORK. Menlo Park, California: Crisp Publications, Inc., 1989.

Smollin, Anne Bryan. JIGGLE YOUR HEART AND TICKLE YOUR SOUL. Latham, New York: Canticle Press, 1994.

TABLE OF CONTENTS

INTRODUCTION

There is a modern story told of the Sufi teacher and holy fool, Mullah Nasrudin. He goes into a bank and tries to cash a check. The teller asks him please to identify himself. Nasrudin reaches into his pocket and pulls out a small mirror. Looking into it, he says, "Yep, that's me all right."

We all need to grow into the kind of awareness and confidence where we know — and are comfortable with — who we are. Sometimes, that is not an easy journey. Sometimes, it takes years. What matters is that we begin that journey and take small steps each day toward our goal.

Father John Powell has a sign on his bathroom mirror (not that I have actually seen it) that reads, "You are looking at the face of the person who is responsible for your happiness today." Perhaps mirror companies should engrave that message on every looking-glass they make. It would be such a help to all of us. It would be a daily reminder that "You" and "I" are responsible for our own happiness.

Life has taught us, wrongly, that everything is easy. If we have a pain, we take a pill. If we need cash, we use our credit cards or an ATM machine. If we have only a few minutes to cook dinner, we use our microwaves. Cellular phones, E-mail and personal beepers allow us instant contact with other people. As a result, when it takes work, thought or investment of self to get something accomplished, we find ourselves looking at a concrete wall (rather than in a mirror) and thinking that the task is too difficult or even impossible.

But happiness and joy are within our reach. They are gifts and blessings and words spoken — and, yes, even unspoken. The problem is not that this state of happiness is unreachable or beyond us. The problem is that we wait for someone else to give it to us, to create our happiness and pleasure.

A Chinese proverb says: "A person without a smiling face must not open a shop." That makes sense: A smile creates warmth, hospitality and openness. Hence, a shop owner with a smile is more successful than a glum one. Who wants to be waited on by a grumpy salesperson? Who wants to live with a person who is not happy? Who wants to work with someone who is negative?

Perhaps we need to look into our own mirrors and take a hard look at what we see. Perhaps we need to write on our own mirrors: "You are looking at the face of the person who is responsible for your happiness today."

Research tells us if we smile long enough, the smile turns to laughter. We know if we tell ourselves something often enough, we begin to believe it. The same is true for smiles.

This book is meant to help you look into the mirror and be responsible for the person you see there. It's a book meant to be practical and to tell stories. It has two focuses:

• The first is to journal some thoughts and ideas so we can get in touch with some of our internal messages. "Journaling" means writing down our thoughts and memories and dreams and fears. Putting such things down in black-and-white can help us a great deal. For example, research indicates that when cancer patients write about the fear and anxiety they feel, they speed the healing process. Journaling allows us to record our deepest thoughts and emotions, and to keep track of those experiences.

Our emotions are a result of our beliefs and thoughts. If we want to feel better, or if we want to understand ourselves and gain greater insight regarding ourselves, journaling is a means to that end. Dr. Bernie Siegel equates journal writing with meditation, asserting that a journal or diary "makes us aware how active our minds are while we're paying no attention to our thoughts, as we shower or eat. A diary can help us become conscious of all these ideas and learn from them." And so we journal.

• This book's second focus is to go outside of ourselves and do something for others that connects us. Just as it is important to internalize and be aware of our emotional world in journaling, it is also important to remember the need to create actions that lead to health and happiness.

Accordingly, this book has been designed with alternating chapters: for example, chapter one is followed by a suggested activity while the second chapter is followed by a journaling activity — including space for you to write. And so on throughout the book.

In the Koran, it is written: "They deserve paradise who make their companions laugh." What life and energy we give to others, and what energy and life others can give to us. We ease one another's burdens and carry one another's sorrows. We share one another's loads.

There is a wonderful old Russian tale about the inhabitants of heaven and hell. They both sit at tables loaded with delicious food. The ground rules for the feast are simple: The diners must eat with extremely long-handed forks, and they must grasp the forks at the end of the handle. The people in hell starve because they cannot figure out how to feed themselves that way. But, for the people in heaven, this is not a problem. They simply reach across the table and feed each other.

When we realize that we were created to be social beings, that we need others and others need us, then we find fullness in life. We become aware of the connectedness of all things: the earth, the sun, the moon, the stars, the grass, the water, the dirt, the animals, the persons we know and those we have not yet had the opportunity to meet. Nothing is separate. When we experience that awareness, we find ourselves praising all living and non-living things. Then we are not just experiencing joy, but extending that joy to others. The connectedness of life goes on.

How true it is that we get ourselves so busy and into so many "things" and activities that we do not take the time to see the presence of the joy right in front of us. Alice Walker paints with her words that reminder in her novel, "The Color Purple":

At one point, Celie and Shug are in earnest conversation about God when Shug corrects Celie's vision of how God manages the universe. Life is not, as Celie thinks, a matter of scurrying about doing good deeds to earn God's approval. It is, rather, taking time to notice, appreciate, and praise what God has provided for our pleasure and enjoyment. "I think it pisses God off if you walk by the color purple in a field somewhere and don't notice it," Shug counsels.

The balance of noticing and recording our thoughts and emotions in journals, and then remembering our connectedness to others is the purpose of this little book. Use it for your own personal growth. Use it in groups for discussion.

My wish is that every time you look in a mirror, you see a person who smiles at you and then takes that smile and warms the world you touch daily.

I need to thank many people for helping get this book to you. To Jim Breig, my editor, who patiently urges me to "keep going." To Kathy Rooke, who takes the superlatives I write and makes them readable. To Etta Jones, my administrative assistant at Counseling for Laity, and Sister Mary Theresa Murphy, CSJ, my bookkeeper and "right hand," for all their encouragement. To Patricia St. John, CSJ, and Janet Cavanaugh, CSJ, who are always there for me.

And, to my Mom, Irma Smollin, and to my sister, Kay Smollin, who have taught me how to selflessly love and give. This book is for YOU.

Chapter One

NEW BEGINNINGS

N ew Year's Day comes around not only so we begin a new calendar year but also to remind us of the importance of new beginnings. The birth of a baby, your first car, the infatuation of a new relationship — all touch us with a breath of fresh air. Beginnings are always filled with a wild variety of emotions. There is always an element of excitement and surprise. The unknown contains an aspect of mystery! There is also a bit of fear and apprehension in the newness. It's like being on untested waters.

Some make New Year's resolutions. They promise this is the year to lose weight or to exercise more or to change some piece of their lives that needs to be addressed. Of course, this is psychologically addressed with great gusto on the first day of a new year. But, ah, how that fervor disappears!

We attend to a new relationship so very differently also. We call the person a million times a week and think of her three million times a day. We buy special cards and gifts, and include him in every inch of our lives. And then, not too long later, we ask, "Whatever happened to what's her name?"

Perhaps all this is necessary so we can avoid ruts

and deep grooves that keep us stuck. Maybe we can be comfortable with whatever we have resolved to address in our lives this year, and, if in 365 days, we can claim "success," fine. If we find, however, that our enthusiasm has not carried us through, we can also see the "success" in at least trying something new.

Beginnings have an enthusiasm that brings life and energy. They allow us to see situations with fresh-ness and breadth. Nothing is too big to tackle. Noth-ing can stop us. Our visions are far-reaching and limitless. The energy is filled with balloons and rain-bows, and we see numerous opportunities to give our new endeavor some of our time and attention.

Action Today: Let me just enjoy the new feeling of energy and direct a few moments in bringing a touch of newness to someone special in my life:

- Hug someone.
- Call someone and tell her you were thinking of her.
- Write a note to someone.
- Tell someone you love him.

Chapter Two

DRAGON BOAT RACES

R ecently, I had the opportunity to go to China. It was truly a marvelous experience. While I was in Taipei, the Dragon-Boat Festival occurred. This exciting and colorful event is very meaningful to the people of China. It was evident from all the people who were lining the river bank that this was a holiday people attended each year.

The custom of the Dragon-Boat Festival centers around the story of Chu Yuan (340-278 B.C.), a counselor to the king of the state of Chu in a turbulent period in Chinese history known as the Era of the Warring States. Chu was a very loyal courtier and a talented man of letters. He wanted to help his king do a better job of governing his country. He was very much trusted and respected by the king.

Then some courtiers became jealous and began to speak ill of Chu. The king listened to these maligners and began to distance himself from his loyal courtier. Chu was completely ignored by the king. Even though he wrote poems to express his feelings to the king, he was exiled. Chu's departure from the capital was soon followed by the annexation of his country by the Chin state. When Chu heard of this, he was so saddened that he committed suicide by jumping into the Milo River.

When Chu's neighbors and friends heard about his suicide, they tried to rescue him by rowing boats to where he had disappeared under the water. Having failed, they then tried to save his body from being devoured by the fish and threw balls of rice wrapped in seaweed into the water in hopes the fish would eat that mixture instead of their friend's body.

Perhaps the story of Chu Yuan is only a legend. Yet, the Chinese value it. The legend that people tried to save Chu Yuan by immediately going over the place where he drowned eventually evolved into the Dragon-Boat Festival. The belief that the people threw balls of rice into the river to feed the fish created the custom of making "tsung tsu," a clump of glutinous rice with meat and egg yolk wrapped in bamboo leaves.

We can learn much from this legend. Chu was passionate in what he valued and believed. The rejection by the king with the mistrust that grew was a betrayal for him. The core of Chu Yuan was wounded and scarred beyond the point of his being able to see that he had other options. For him, having his sincerity challenged was beyond belief. Chu attempted to express himself through his poetry, but the words went unheard by the king. This was the ultimate devastation for the loyal servant.

Reflect on a time when you felt your sincerity or integrity was being questioned. Write your feelings here:

What resulted?

How has this influenced who you are now?

How did this incident help you to get to know and believe in yourself more?

What did you become aware of that you didn't like about yourself?

Chu Yuan was passionate in his beliefs and values. What are your passions?

For Chu, the rejection of the king and the mistrust that grew was a betrayal. What is your reaction when you feel rejected?

Chapter Three

LOVING ONESELF

"To love oneself is the beginning of a life-long romance" — Oscar Wilde

Maybe it's a whole new idea to begin to care and attend to the person I look at in the mirror. How do I get rid of the old message that keeps running through my head that to think about myself first is selfish? How can I learn that I have to have that level of respect and dignity for myself in order to be able to give the same respect and dignity to another?

Every time I grow into an awareness of one of my own gifts or talents, I enrich my world and those with whom I come into contact. I also take one more step for myself toward wholeness.

Action Today: Every hour today, I am going to take one minute and tell myself one positive thing about myself. I am going to acknowledge one of my gifts or remind myself of the good deeds or random acts of kindness I do.

Before I put my head on my pillow tonight, I am going to stand in front of a mirror and repeat the messages I have learned or re-learned today — and then smile at myself as I remember that I am a good person, and I am capable and lovable.

Chapter Four

WHEN THINGS ARE NOT THE WAY YOU WANT THEM

I have a wonderful little girl in my life who always brings me joy and happiness. She helps me keep things in perspective. Children have a way of gracing our lives with reality and balance.

Lesley was born with an abundant supply of self-esteem. Truly, she has more than an average person needs to get through life successfully. She seems to go merrily to each new task and to bring to it a new supply of energy and enthusiasm. Fear is not part of her vocabulary or thought process. She is always eager to learn something new, and her every task becomes a new experience that makes life a bit fuller.

Lesley's brother Stephen is not blessed with the same degree of self-esteem. He questions himself a lot more, is a bit more hesitant to try new things, and wonders about the outcome of a projected task before he even begins it. Stephen, however, is a gifted saxophone player who could challenge many mature and trained musicians. Yet, when he was asked to play his sax in a Christmas play for the high school, Stephen, who was only eight, did not view this request as an honor. To him, it was a scary and terrifying task.

He was out in the car with my sister, who is his godmother, and Lesley. Stephen began questioning my sister: "What if I make a mistake during the concert?"

My sister assured him immediately, "Stephen, you will be fine. Don't worry about a thing."

Stephen continued, "But what if I make a mistake?"

My sister quickly responded, "It doesn't matter, Stephen. We are all so proud of you. Don't worry about it."

Stephen said a bit louder, "Yeah, but what if I make a mistake?"

Lesley was in the back seat of the car, listening to her eight-year-old brother. Even though she was only four, she never questioned whether she had the right to get involved in this intimate conversation.

"Stephen," the voice from the back seat began, "do you remember when I was in the ballet recital? What happened? I fell down right in the middle of it. And what did I do, Stephen? I picked myself up and started all over again. Now, Stephen, just pick yourself up and start all over again."

The wise solution was evident to a four-year-old who was gifted with the confidence not to get stuck in a mistake or failure. She didn't even get stuck in the event. Somehow, she "just picked herself up and started all over again." No mess! No hesitation! No doubting! No wondering about what others were thinking!

Sometimes, we all need to have a Lesley in the back seat. We need to hear, "Just pick yourself up and start all over again."

Easy? No way! But the energy and freedom lie in picking ourselves up and starting all over.

Reflect on an incident when something did not go the way you had planned. What were your feelings?

What did you learn about yourself?

How are you different today because of that event or experience?

Write about other times you've "picked yourself up and started all over again."

Try to become aware of what you would not have experienced or would not have learned if you hadn't risked trying again.

Chapter Five

LAUGH OFTEN

L aughter tickles and brings life to our souls. When we laugh with another person, we are bonded with her and grow closer. Laughter energizes our whole body. The effects of laughter can stay with us for at least 45 minutes.

Doesn't it make sense to choose something that gives life and energy to us so we can benefit from the effects that remain in our bodies? It doesn't cost any money, and you don't have to buy any special clothes or join a club. To find laughter in the present moment requires only our desire to find it. Laughter is ever-present. But if I have blinders on, I limit my vision and cannot find the gift of joy that is there.

Action Today:

☐ I will give myself a laughter break.

☐ I'll find someone and enjoy the gift of laughter with him.

☐ I'll make a phone call to someone who has the ability to help me laugh, and then hold on to that memory and enjoy that gift throughout the day.

☐ I'll consciously look for the humorous moments

that are in front of me and celebrate them with a good belly laugh.

Chapter Six

LAUGHTER: THE SOUL'S MEDICINE

T he benefits of laughter are numerous. We can opt to become more open, healthy and creative people by assuring we keep laughter in our lives.

We exercise our organs when we laugh. (It sure beats jogging!) We create community and feel bonded with people with whom we laugh. We tend to share more with these people and are more comfortable in their presence.

Laughter has to become as important as eating and breathing. Just as we need food to keep our bodies alive, we need laughter to keep our hearts healthy and our souls vibrant. When we can laugh, we tend to see options that are available to us that get blocked and distorted when we don't laugh. It is this visible laughter that helps us enrich our sense of humor.

Humor is a grace. It lets us work more effectively and play more enthusiastically. It gives us the courage to change and creates the balance for us to deal effectively with difficulties. Humor teaches us to be creatively flexible. It is a way of seeing ourselves and others, a way of dealing with serious issues in our lives.

Laughter doesn't mean we do not deal with difficulties or never feel hurt or sad or cry. Far from it! When we have this sense of humor, we are free enough to be able to feel the sorrow that leads to tears.

Laughter gives us the ability to laugh at what might otherwise terrify us. It lets us face the fears that could suffocate us. Laughter really diminishes physical and psychological pain. And to think this gift is within each of us and is free (no prescriptions needed)!

Laughter has some physical payoffs. It strengthens heart muscles and lowers blood pressure. It even improves face value!

Reflect on times when laughter has been present in your life.

Who are the people with whom you laugh and share the grace of humor?

What are other things that help you laugh?

Make a plan of action to put into each day one act of your choice that helps you laugh. Make a contract with yourself to do that.

Chapter Seven

NO NEED TO BE PERFECT

I want to remember positive things I recalled about myself, and I want to start to love myself and what I am and what I do. That means I have to remember that while I still have some rough edges, they don't make me bad.

Human beings aren't perfect. And that's all I am — a human being. So why do I expect more of myself than of others? I need to remember that human beings trip and fall, say things they sometimes don't mean, and make mistakes. Those are not really failures. They are ruts and grooves that we need to grow into an awareness of. Then we see them as they are. Not as nooses around our necks or utter failures or weaknesses in our personalities, but as things that human beings need to attend to and be aware of so that we may also allow others to be that human in their own lives.

Loving ourselves means loving even our rough edges. That doesn't mean we never address these issues or behaviors but that we see them for what they are — traits of being human.

Action Today: I am not going to put myself down for making a mistake. I am going to laugh at the times I trip, make a mistake or make a choice I wish I hadn't made.

As I laugh at those moments today, I will be aware of other choices I can make and try to decrease the rough edges — not by putting myself down but by staying aware that I can do things differently.

Keep score. How many mistakes can you make today? Make at least five and anything over that will be bonus points. Here's hoping you have a high score.

Chapter Eight

LABELS DEFINE US

 Have you ever noticed that we often speak in sentences that don't use a universal vocabulary?

Everything today has been reduced to a symbol, a label. We begin to refer to ourselves and others using those labels, and they form a message system that is loaded with judgments and interpretations which may or may not be accurate. For example, it is not uncommon to hear talk of ACOA; NA; AA; SLAA; SAA; OA; NF; NT; SJ; SP; a number on the Enneagram; and words like "dysfunctional" and "co-dependent." They are commonly used in both professional environments and in casual conversation at cocktail parties.

For some people, such labels become a status symbol. People begin to define and think of themselves in terms of the initials. Then there is another whole set of initials that establish academic criteria: B.S., B.A., M.S., M.A., Ph.D. There are other labels as well: divorced, widowed, single-parent, blended parent family, step-parent family, lesbian, gay. Some labels indicate professions: lawyer, doctor, teacher, priest, sister, accountant, banker, author, humorist, commentator, meteorologist.

And, of course, we have traditional roles that have

been given label names: mother, father, siblings, brother, sister, grandparents, aunt, uncle, cousin. We also associate according to race and ethnic categories: Black, Caucasian, Hispanic and Native American. The list goes on and on.

We must not get caught in labels. Labels are like houses. We often see only the exterior of the house. Hence, our information of what's inside is very limited. Not until we are allowed into a home can we understand what it's all about. We can get to know the identity of the house by the number of rooms, the style of the wallpaper, the paint colors, the pictures on the wall, the furniture. All of that is a mystery until we are inside.

People are like that, too. We see them so differently once we know them. We learn personality traits and interests. We learn what they like and dislike, and how they enjoy spending their free time. They become personal to us and are no longer described in physical terms or by a label.

Often, our awareness changes as we get to know another person better. First impressions are frequently incorrect. Labels do not identify who this person really is. If we view someone as an ACOA, we may be quick to judge that he will be afraid of intimacy and will be aloof. If we judge one to be co-dependent, we may misjudge a friendship or support system. The fault is in the label.

Labels have a way of keeping us stuck in the past. It is like tying a noose around our necks and never realizing we can do things differently tomorrow. Yesterdays certainly will always influence us. However, if yesterdays control us, we are never free. Labels can create un-freedoms.

List as many labels as you can that refer to you.

Which of these do you accept?

Which have you chosen to hold on to so you can opt not to have to change?

What labels have you put on others?

What effect have these labels had on your relationships with others?

How have labels limited the way you have gotten to know another person?

Chapter Nine

EXPECTATIONS

 L et's call today "Choose to be Happy Day!" That would help us remember three things:

1. That happiness is a choice;

2. That not all people choose to be happy; and

3. That it takes practice for some people to learn #1.

Do you think that some people are born to be happy while others are not? That's like believing that some people are born good and others are created evil. Do you believe it is another person's fault that you are not happy? It isn't. That's why we need a day to remind ourselves:

• That my happiness is MY happiness; and

• That happiness doesn't come from someone else or because of someone else.

It is certainly true that we live within a network of people who influence us, a network that includes our family, friends, colleagues, people with whom we worship and our neighbors. We have expectations for all of them — and they have expectations for us. Sometimes, those expectations are rational and consistent. At other times, they are irrational or contradictory.

When we become disappointed or upset with ourselves or others, it is usually because our expectations are not met. Sometimes, we must re-think and change them. To hold on to an unreasonable expectation only keeps us hurt or angry — and unhappy.

Action Today: When I start to feel upset or frustrated, I'll check out what I was expecting. If I shared the expectation with the other person, I need either to bring it back up or decide to change it. I want to choose my own happiness, and holding on to an expectation that is irrational is to set myself up for more hurt and unhappiness.

If I did not share the expectation with the other, I will begin there. If the response from the other is that she cannot live with the expectation or that it is unfair, then I will change it.

Chapter Ten

OTHERS SOMETIMES TELL US WHO WE ARE

Many people never take the time to learn who they are. They live off the messages of those who tell them that they are good or not good, that they can achieve certain things or that they have failed.

Some spend a lifetime as strangers to themselves. To be happy, whole persons, we must be free enough:

- to know ourselves...

- to look in a mirror and choose to like what we see...

- to own our strengths and our weaknesses...

- to attend to our needs, and to nourish our bodies and minds...

- to hear what others say about us.

Jean-Paul Sartre claimed, "Freedom is what you do with what's been given to you." Eleanor Roosevelt reminded us: "No one can make you feel inferior without your consent." Why would we give that much power to anyone else? Why do we give charge of ourselves to others?

It is essential to our happiness that we respect and

accept ourselves. That doesn't mean we won't have a few things about us that are not perfect and that we won't like. It does mean, however, that we have a sense of integrity and self-worth.

There is a benefit in listening to others and hearing what they are saying about us. We cannot truly know and accept who we are unless others take the time to tell us. We need others in our lives, and we need others to affirm us. That validates us. Without affirmation, we will never be able to know ourselves.

Still, many of us only hear the negative things that are said or remember only the rejections. People hold on to those messages for years without choosing to listen to them or deciding what to do with them. Some need just to be discarded. Others need to be heard to provide us feedback so that we may make different choices and appropriate changes in our lives.

List five people who have been very influential in your life:

1.

2.

3.

4.

5.

For each person listed, write two sentences that they would use to describe you as a person:

1A.

1B.

2A.

2B.

3A.

3B.

4A.

4B.

5A.

5B.

Write a paragraph that you would send to someone who had to pick you up at the airport and had never met you. Describe who you are so you can be identified.

Reread that paragraph and be sure it does not convey a negative image of who you are. Rewrite it if necessary.

List the three strongest and most positive things about you:

1.

2.

3.

List three things you would like to change about yourself:

1.

2.

3.

How can you change them? Write one specific thing that would allow you to change them:

Chapter Eleven

STAR GAZING

J anuary 6 — "Little Christmas" — is the day that the Three Kings arrived at the stable, bringing their gifts to the Baby Jesus. It is also the feast that honors that great star that led the Magi to the Christ child.

January 6 can be a day for us to remember the "stars" in our lives: the people and the messages that have led us to where we are and to whom we have become.

As we look back over our lives, we remember those who have touched us with their influence and guidance. We recall situations that led us to other situations. Some of these are not happy memories; they are very painful recalls:

☐ It is sad to remember people we have loved who are no longer in our lives because they have died or have chosen not to be part of our lives any more.

☐ It is sad to recall things that have not worked out as we planned.

But those messages — those stars — led us to something and perhaps provided a path that was bright enough for us to walk on. Blessings come to us in strange ways!

Action Today: Spend a few moments gazing at the stars tonight. Enjoy the vast and awesome sight of our universe. As you gaze at our galaxy, remember the personal "stars" in your own life. Be grateful for their presence and for the influence with which they touched your life.

Chapter Twelve

LETTING GO

 oday is all we have that is real.
We cannot change the past.
We cannot take back a word we've said.
We cannot redo a thing we've done.

The only thing we can change is the way we feel about the past.

We do not have a lot of control over the future either. We can plan for tomorrow and hope our plans are actualized, but we cannot make everything happen our way.

Yet so many of us are controlled by our yesterdays and tomorrows. As a result, we lose our todays. There is no energy in our past or in our future. Our energy is grounded in the present.

Thinking back on painful experiences is like living the experience again:

It is giving to the experience a lot more power than necessary.

It is keeping the situation or experience alive.

You really are hurting yourself when you choose to hold on to those memories. You are empowering the past but not empowering the present. As you stay stuck in that memory, you exhaust yourself.

Does it change it to relive it over and over for years? Of course not. The only thing it does is keep you out of touch with now and the opportunities right in front of you so that you are not truly living. It is never too late to cut those nooses off our necks and toss them away.

Some people hold on to childhood memories and beliefs, allowing them to define who they are.

Maybe you didn't feel smart enough or loved enough as a child. Does that mean you have to dislike yourself forever?

Are those your excuses so you can behave inappropriately?

Does that justify your moodiness or your lack of communication with others?

Holding on to negative thoughts and experiences only gives us a negative view of life. Unfortunately, others get victimized by such actions and words of ours.

Forgiving our past and letting go of what drains us is opting for fully living each moment. At times, this forgiving needs to be ritualized by going to another person and asking for forgiveness. Old feelings that are deeply imbedded in us need to be resurfaced, owned and then replaced with other feelings.

If you have hurt someone else, it may be necessary to go to that person and ask for forgiveness.

If it is not possible to do that in person, then you

may have to do it in your thoughts. Have a conversation with the other, resolve those feelings, and then let go of them.

The next step is forgiving yourself. That's not always easy. It is not easy to forgive, let go and move on. But the alternative is to let the other person continue to hurt you or to continue to let yourself be hurt. To break the cycle of pain, you must be in control of yourself and not let another be in control of you.

There is a wonderful story of how monkeys are caught in Asia. There is a specific kind of monkey that searches for a special kind of nut to eat. The people create a box with a hole in the front and place that nut inside. When the monkey smells the nut, it reaches inside to grab it. Once the monkey has the nut in its fist, it cannot get its hand out of the hole because its clenched hand is too wide for the opening.

All the monkey has to do is let go of the nut so it could pull its hand out of the box and be free.

But the monkey holds on to the nut and is captured.

We hold on to things, too, instead of letting them go and freeing ourselves. These "un-freedoms" are our hurts and disappointments. They keep us from believing in ourselves and hold us back in nurturing who we are. We do not see ourselves as we are.

We are always changing.

We need to value who we are and who we can become.

We need to be gentle with ourselves and to respect ourselves.

We need to let go of the past and to forgive.

Forgiveness is a conscious act. It is not a feeling. We never have to agree the other was right or grow into an agreement of a painful event. We just need to be in control of ourselves and choose life.

Recall a past situation that was hurtful to you. Choose one in which you felt rejected or uncounted. Write down that situation.

List all the feelings you had at that time.

What did you want to happen?

How was it healed? If it was never healed, is there any way you can resolve it for yourself now?

What are other things you hold on to and to whom do you give that control?

Contract with yourself to let go of one of the above and specifically write down what you can do to be in control.

Do you need to ask anyone else for forgiveness?

How can you take action and responsibility for this?

Are you holding on to a childhood image or memory that defines you negatively?

How can you let go of the past and not continue to hurt yourself the way you've let others hurt you?

Write a letter to someone telling that person you forgive him or her for whatever happened in your life. Write and write and write. (Spelling does not count.

You are never going to send it.) After you have written
it, reread it and write down what you have learned.

Chapter Thirteen

TAKE A RISK

S ometimes, we don't experience happiness in our lives because we don't risk enough to find it. We do the same things over and over again. We confine ourselves to activities that we think might make us happy. We repeat the same old things year after year, and feel safe and comfortable.

But we never reexamine or try something new or create a new hobby or relationship or pattern in our life that brings excitement. So boredom and complacency become characteristic of our life. They are really negative enemies of happiness.

Action Today: Do something out of your normal routine:

- Greet a stranger with a compliment.

- Invite a person to whom you don't owe anything to dinner.

- Drive to work a different way.

- Call a person you know would love to hear from you.

- Jot a note to a lonely person or to someone who

lives alone.

- Wear something to work that you have never worn before.

- Spend half the day at a museum.

- Go for a drive to a place you have never been before.

Do something that expands your comfort zone and feel the pleasure that comes from opening yourself to a new experience.

Chapter Fourteen

GRIEVING AND LOSS

O ne of the most difficult things we have to deal with is facing the illness or death of someone we love. Our world changes instantly. It becomes focused on that person; all priorities are measured in relation to the loss we are experiencing (or are about to experience).

Our bodies ache with pain....Our emotions are caught in our throats....Emptiness becomes a companion....Our actions become unconscious, and we go through our day routinely and robot-like....Things that used to mean a great deal are no longer important....People who could once tap our sense of humor no longer can reach us....Isolation feels safe....Depression offers security.

We begin to question everything and everyone:

☐ Why is this person sick?

☐ What is death?

☐ Why does anyone ever have to suffer?

☐ Is there really a God? Certainly God could never be kind and loving or it would never hurt this bad, we say.

Ignoring pain does not make it go away. We just

transfer our feelings and possibly make things worse. Facing our feelings is not always an easy thing. But feelings are not right or wrong, and they will not hurt us. It helps if we can talk about this pain with someone we trust.

It tears us apart when we have to deal with the loss of our loved one. Sickness leaves everyone helpless:

☐ The unknown is always in front of us.

☐ Thoughts go through our heads at such a rate that we can hardly remember them and certainly cannot make any sense of them.

☐ We are angry at our own helplessness in not being able to aid the other.

☐ We are angry at the other for getting sick.

☐ Then the circle widens, and we get angry at everyone. We even get mad at ourselves, asking: Why is this happening? Why can't we do anything about it?

We search for someone who can do something, but we can't find that person. We feel alone and isolated in our pain. Despair is close to us. We even begin to breathe differently. Our breathing becomes quite shallow. We decrease the amount of oxygen in our lungs and feel a lack of life in our bodies.

The thought of living without this significant person in our life is just too overwhelming. We wonder, "How does anyone ever fill that empty space? Why would we ever want anyone to fill that space anyway?"

I was in the Philadelphia airport one time, enjoying

a Pepsi and hot dog. I always treat myself to a photography magazine when I'm traveling and devour it while munching a hot dog. On this occasion, a man asked to share the table I was at. I moved my things closer to me to give him some space. He then looked at me and said, out of the blue: "I don't believe in God!"

I looked around to see who he was talking to and realized it was me. I said, "You don't believe in God?" He responded, "No."

I wondered why he was sharing this with me. There were thousands of people in the airport. Why me? I didn't know the man. I was dressed in slacks and a shirt, and had no sign over my head that read: "Come talk to me. I'm lonely."

I needed to decide whether I was going to continue my ritual of eating my hot dog, drinking my Pepsi and reading my photography magazine, or put that agenda aside and listen to this stranger for a few minutes. I closed my book. He then told me his story:

He had a daughter who was very ill. The man was very wealthy and could afford any medical treatment for his daughter, but there was nothing anyone could do. To make matters worse, his daughter's husband was a doctor and his skills were not enough. This elderly gentleman said he had tested God by standing in front of a bush at his house waiting for it to burst into flames. It never did!

I listened as he relayed his despair and hopelessness. As we finished our "supper," he concluded: "I still don't believe there is a God. If there were a God, my daughter would be cured. If there were a God, the bush in front of my house would be in flames. If there were a God, there would be no calories in hot fudge sundaes."

As I walked away, I knew a bit more about him. He was no longer a stranger. He was anonymous, but he had shared his story and his pain. He was vulnerable. And my heart was touched by his hurt and pain.

I walked to the gate from which I was departing and carried the man with me. My thoughts were back at the table we had shared. I remembered the look in his eyes. I was grateful I had made the choice to listen for a few minutes to this stranger rather than continue the ritual of reading my photography magazine.

A few minutes later, he appeared by my side and offered me some candy.

How did he find me?

Where was he going?

By some chance was he going on the same flight as I?

Again, I closed my book, realizing this conversation could go on only a few minutes since I would be boarding the plane soon. We also had assigned seats, so he would have to finish soon.

As the rows were called to board the plane, I said goodbye for the second time to this hurting man. Immediately on getting into my seat, I took out my photography magazine. Now it was time for me. I would read every word of it.

Only a few seconds passed before the person assigned to the seat next to me arrived. Guess who it was?

Right! The very same gentleman. Now I was beginning to question whether there is a God!

Again, I was confronted with the choice to read my magazine or listen. I closed my book, and he talked and talked and talked. I only listened.

As we landed in Albany an hour later, he turned and told me how good he felt: "No one has let me talk through this. Everyone wants me to feel better immediately. They all tell me how I should or shouldn't feel. You only listened. Thank you."

While walking down the aisle to exit the plane, he realized he had never told me his name. After he introduced himself, he asked my name.

"Sister Anne Bryan Smollin," I responded.

"You're a nun?" he said incredulously. "I told a nun I didn't believe in God!"

He turned to the gentleman across the aisle and said, "She's a nun, and I told her I didn't believe in God!" Others looked puzzled. Some smiled. Fearful we were going to get the entire plane into this personal discussion, I found myself inching my way off the plane.

"Do you need a ride some place?" my new friend asked.

"No, thank you," I answered. "My mother is going to pick me up."

After I greeted my Mom, we walked toward the baggage claim area. The gentleman came over to my Mom. "You have a wonderful daughter," he said.

Mom responded, "Thank you. I think she is wonderful, too."

After walking a few more yards, Mom asked me, "Who is he?"

I answered: "I don't know. Someone who said he doesn't believe there is a God."

"But you told him there was, didn't you?" she asked.

"No," I said. "He already knows."

That wasn't good enough for Mom. "You go right over there," she ordered, "and tell him there is a God!"

So many times, I've thought about that man. His loss was so great. He was so helpless. His pain was defining him. There was a huge emptiness surrounding his every thought. Everything he looked at reminded him of his dying daughter.

Write about a loss that devastated you.

Write all the feelings you remember having and still may have regarding that loss.

Who were the people you told about the situation?

What behaviors did you find yourself exhibiting at that time?

What is it like for you now?

What did you learn from that experience?

Chapter Fifteen

GIFT GIVING

homas a Kempis wrote: "A wise lover values not so much the gift of the lover as the love of the giver."

It's really what is in our hearts and the motivation behind our actions that count with someone else. Material possessions have value only because of the meaning held in the heart of the giver.

Sometimes, we struggle with choosing the appropriate gift for a person. Some spend hours shopping and searching for the "right" gift. But did you ever watch a person open a card and cherish every word inside? Nothing inside except warm feelings of caring and love and concern. How do you put a price tag on those?

Can you recall when you received a phone call from a person you hadn't heard from in a long time. How does one count the cost of that gift?

Action Today: Give something away. I'm not talking about a material possession. I'm suggesting that you give a smile to someone...or speak a kind word to someone...or write a note to a person that lives alone.

Pick up a phone and say something that will bring a smile to another's face. And watch the way that smile will remain in your heart all day.

Chapter Sixteen

NOT FITTING IN

There are times you just don't feel you fit. You try your best. But when you compare yourself with others and the way they dress and wear their hair and the kinds of cars they drive, you feel inferior. You begin to question your value and self-worth. Everyone seems so competent. No one else makes mistakes or messes up things quite as much as you do.

It's hard to surface positive things about ourselves. No one seems to state anything worthwhile or positive when we need to hear it. And even if they do, we just don't hear it.

Sometimes, we try to fit in places that really are not for us. Many stay in those places for years, and are frustrated and depressed. No matter what you do, it doesn't change a thing. You just don't fit. You are different.

Maybe we need to begin to look at ourselves and not at another person or the situation in which we find ourselves. That takes a lot of honesty and sincerity. It is also very risky. If is isn't right, then it may mean we have to leave, do something else, or go another place. How frightening!

There is a wonderful Chinese fable about a man from the state of Lu who was very skilled in weaving hemp sandals and about his wife who was very adept at weaving fine silk. The couple decided to move to the state of Yue in the south.

"You will be in dire straits," the man was told.

"Why?" asked the man of Lu.

"Hemp sandals are for walking, but the people of Yue walk barefoot. Silk is used for making hats, but the people of Yue go bare-headed. If you go to a place where your skills are utterly useless, how can you hope to do well?"

Like the couple from Lu, we sometimes put ourselves in situations that set us up for failure. It's like seeing the forest and not knowing anything about the trees or what lives in the environment. People say they are like "a fish out of water." We often hear people talk about relatives in their family who are not like anyone else and "no one knows who they take after."

We hear people talk about views and opinions they have and then add, "No one understands me." It's like speaking a different language. Judgments are made about others when we see them through our eyes. The perception may be way off. But to the one holding it, it is real and solid.

The Chinese tell a fable about a man who lost his axe. This man suspected his neighbor's son of stealing it. To him, everything about this boy — the expression on his face, the way he walked, his speech patterns — betrayed that he had stolen the axe.

Not too long afterwards, the man found the axe while rummaging through his cellar. The next time he saw his neighbor's son, nothing about the boy's behavior or appearance seemed to suggest the boy had stolen the axe.

What changed?

Our opinions and judgments seem to fit for us, but they are sometimes a bit off base. It is with openness and the ability to see more than one option that we grow. Our blurred vision hampers and stifles us. But change is not easy. It can even be painful!

There is a story about an old man who lived beside a very busy intersection and named his servant boy "Fighter" and his dog "Biter." For three or four years, no one ever came to visit him. The old man wondered why and began asking. Someone finally told him the truth. When he changed the name of the servant boy and the dog, he had a stream of visitors.

What if that man had never asked? What if he had chosen to live in his little enclosed world. He would have deprived himself of life and laughter.

What changed?

Think of a situation where you were asked to change something. Write about the situation.

What was it like to struggle and put forth the effort to change?

Who helped you see what you needed to do?

How was the message given to you?

What would be different for you if you never listened to that message?

How have you tried to learn from that?

Chapter Seventeen

LOVE MISCHIEF

When we can laugh at ourselves, we help ourselves and others to relax. Laughter relaxes our muscles, and the need to be perfect disappears very quickly. We find ourselves becoming childlike, and it just feels good to exercise our organs with the energy of our laughter.

Friedrich Nietzsche said, "To laugh means to love mischief." Mischief is so often limited to the world of a child and barred from the adult world. Yet mischief makes us alive and likeable and creative. The wonderful thing about mischief is that it cannot be enjoyed alone, so we immediately get connected with others. Now, two worlds and two hearts and two souls are touched with new life.

Action Today: Be mischievous:

☐ Throw a snowball or make a snowman.

☐ Write a letter to Santa Claus and thank him for last year's Christmas gifts.

☐ Send flowers to someone and don't sign your name.

☐ Invite someone to dinner, cook a brand new

recipe, and risk having it come out edible.

☐ Get into trouble — not serious trouble but trouble that causes laughter for yourself and another.

Chapter Eighteen

A CHORUS LINE

Broadway shows are wonderful experiences. They entertain and even bring us to tears. Melodies of the songs heard in Broadway shows are sung over and over, finding places in our lives.

"A Chorus Line," the longest-running Broadway show, is my very favorite. The play was not like the usual Broadway spectacular. Usually, you go to Broadway shows to see the gorgeous scenery and costumes as well as to be exposed to the plot of the play. "A Chorus Line" was different. There were no costumes. There was no scenery. The play opened on an empty stage with a lot of nervous people standing there waiting to audition for a spot on the chorus line. Each person was living in her or his own world and telling herself or himself how much she or he needed this job.

Within the first ten minutes of the play, the director dismisses half of the participants and then tells the remaining group how he is going to pick the final chorus line. Each is told to stand on the white line drawn across the stage. When their names are called, they step forth and tell him who they are. He wants to know everything about them. Not just their age and where they come from but everything they had ever done in life — good things and bad things. And based on that, he picks the chorus line. Then the director comes and sits in the audience. It is only then that one can see the mirrors on the backstage wall. Now the audience could feel part of this play, too.

The director calls the first person. She gives her name, says that she is 22 and comes from San Francisco, and has six brothers. She continues to mime her story.

Another nervous participant walks out and asks the audience, "What do I say? If I tell him I stole all that stuff, I'll never get the job. But if I don't tell him and he finds out, I won't get the job. What do I say?" And he continues to tell us his story.

Then the director calls another dancer. He steps forward, yells his name and begins giving his data. Again, in mime. Another anxious interviewee steps out of line. He asks, "What do I tell him? Do I tell him I'm a homosexual?" He goes on to talk about his life.

The story of "A Chorus Line" is not about the people called forth but about the people who stand on the line and wait, about all those who tell us who they really are and are sometimes frightened they will not be accepted or chosen. This play is about a bunch of real people, people like you and me who stand in front of others and wonder if they will make room for us, wonder if they will accept us.

The play runs two hours and ten minutes without an intermission. Near the end of the play, the director walks out on stage and asks all of them why they want to be in a chorus line. In reality, he explains, the play they are auditioning for won't last forever. It may go a few weeks or a few months or even a few years, but then they will have to get another job.

People began questioning themselves and searching for the values they held in trying to understand why they wanted this job. It is at this point of the play we hear that very beautiful song, "What I Did I Did For Love." How can anyone not get caught up in the message: "Kiss today goodbye, the sweetness and the sorrow. Wish me luck. The same to you. And I won't regret what I did for love, what I did for love...." I remember leaning over to the person I was with and saying, "This is the best show I've ever seen."

Then the director takes charge once more: "All right, now I'm going to pick the chorus line. Everyone come and stand on the white line. As I call your name, please step forth." Slowly, painfully, the director calls half the group forth. He then states, "Second line, you're the chorus line. Report to work on Monday morning."

The rest of the stage members are devastated. I leaned over to the person I was with and said, "This is worst show I've ever seen."

She quickly reminded me, "You just said it was the best."

"I know," I answered, "but it's also the worst."

The story of "A Chorus Line" is the story of us. It's the story of real people who stand in front of others all the time. We tell others who we are and become very vulnerable. It is very risky telling others who we are and what we need. It lets others know things about us that we often hide deep inside.

As the actors walked off the stage, you found yourself totally involved with all of them. You knew who they were and the secrets they had kept locked inside for so long. These people were not strangers. You felt intimately involved with them. You found yourself talking to them:

- "Don't tell that about yourself. No one cares."

- "You're a good person."

- "I'm so glad you shared that with us."

These actors wanted and needed this job. They were passionate in their desire to be hired. They doubted themselves. They revealed themselves. They risked being transparent. And some of them knew they would not be chosen. Some of them knew this risk would be in vain.

Once you tell someone something about you, it is not possible to take it back. Denial is not possible. Once you've been vulnerable, it is never the same again.

What happens to us when we take that risk? What is the result of our soul-searching shared? Or do we chose to remain closed and keep our secrets locked inside for only us to know? It is possible for us never to open up to anyone, but the price is great:

☐ It means we never grow close to another.

☐ It means we lock up inside who we are and never become who we could truly be.

☐ It means we never give birth to parts of us that require risk and sharing and vulnerability.

☐ It means we do not choose life or living.

Think of a time you risked telling another a piece of information about yourself that you never shared with another person. What was it?

What was the reaction of the person you told?

What was your relationship with that person after that?

What did you learn about yourself because of that?

What are some other secrets you keep locked up inside of you and are afraid to disclose to anyone else?

Think of someone who risked sharing some part of himself/herself with you. What was it like for you? Recall how you felt. What was the effect that sharing had on your relationship?

Recall the first time you trusted another. Write about what happened and what you learned from that risk.

Sometimes, other people don't respond the way we would like them to. Sometimes, we feel misunderstood or rejected. There are even situations where we find we have shared a lot about ourselves, perhaps for years, and then the relationship changes or ends. Recall a time that was your reality. Write about what your feelings were and how you felt when the relationship changed.

Chapter Nineteen

MUSIC

Music was first produced by human beings in 25,000 B.C. What would the world be without music? Beethoven, Bach, Chopin and Mozart touch our souls, stir our emotions and bring beauty to our ears.

Besides, what would our children wear to cover their ears if they did not have portable CDs and cassettes? How would we drive our cars without a radio or tape deck? How could we dance our hearts out without a band playing our favorite sentimental songs reminding us of intimate moments we've shared?

Action Today: Give yourself a half hour to listen to your favorite music. Don't do anything else while listening to it. Just HEAR it. Listen to the message of the music. What was the composer saying and what was the gift to us? Listen to one classical piece and one piece that holds a special memory for you. Treat your heart to that special recall. Where would we be without music? How could we hear our soul?

Chapter Twenty

A SPECIAL MEETING

I had the privilege of meeting a Sister of St. Joseph from Lithuania who was very elderly when I first encountered her. Sister Albertina served her God daily. She worked hard and was obedient to her superiors. When she was in the community, all decisions were made by superiors, and any questioning or disagreeing with those decisions was unheard of.

When I was in the Juniorate (a time when we already had taken first vows and were finishing our undergraduate degrees so we could then go out on a teaching assignment), Sister Albertina was our cook. From early morning until late at night, she could be found in the kitchen. Aside from the task of cooking for 135 people for every meal, she would say Rosary after Rosary after Rosary.

Each of us would take our turn to help prepare meals with her. When we reported to the kitchen, Sister Albertina would delegate the tasks so the meal would be completed for the scheduled hour. As we began mixing, stirring and using up the leftovers, Sister Albertina would recite the Rosary aloud. Every so often, she would forget the mystery she was saying and ask, "What decade are we on?"

"Fifth" would always be the response. There are only five, and we hoped she would stop. But she just began the next five decades. Never was there a break from this routine.

Throughout the years, I grew closer to this holy woman, and my mother became her friend, companion and family. Each week, they would visit nursing homes to bring some joy and caring to the residents. Sister Albertina would bring her relics and bless every person she met, whether they wanted it or not. It didn't matter. Neither did she ever consider whether one was Roman Catholic. Everyone got blessed.

When Sister Albertina could no longer go on this weekly venture, my faithful mother continued to visit her friend. The two of them would say the Rosary and the Stations of the Cross together as their relationship grew. When Sister became bedridden, my mother became her secretary and voice as she made Sister's daily telephone calls to shut-ins.

When Sister Albertina was dying, I was asked to come to our Provincial House as quickly as possible since we were her family. One of the sisters with whom I lived accompanied me. As we walked into Sister Albertina's room, it was evident she had only a little more time on earth.

I pulled a chair next to the bed and took her hand. I told her how special she always had been to me (this was nothing new, for I told her this often) and how I always had depended on her prayers. That would never change.

One of her dear friends was then wheeled into the

room: Sister Anna, who was blind and the same age as Sister Albertina. I moved over as they held hands. Sister Anna told her friend of the wonderful years they had shared. She recited some of the difficult moments through which they had supported each other. Although we were listening to a monologue, it was a conversation between two women who had shared life, many happy moments and many incidents of suffering.

Sister Anna then said to all of us present, "Let us say a decade of the Rosary. Which one should we say?"

I froze. The only mysteries I could remember were the fifth. What if she asked me? I sat very quietly waiting for someone to rescue the moment.

"Let's say the Second Joyful Mystery," someone finally offered.

"Ah! The Visitation. When two women met and embraced and nothing was the same again." The wisdom of our elderly Sister Anna!

Some of us have been blessed by meeting someone and nothing ever being the same again. Such friends live forever in our hearts and souls. They are the kind of people who, as soon as they are in view, bring a smile to our face and warmth to our hearts. They are the kind of people who can live in another part of the world but are always near us. Once our life is touched by someone special like that, nothing stays the same.

It's important that we cherish these relationships and nurture them. They are worth more than money or precious jewels. Their very presence is a present. Gifts like that are too valuable not to be protected.

Think of a person has came into your life so that "nothing was ever the same." Write about that person and who he or she is to you.

What are the qualities and values that person possesses that make that person so special to you?

Write three things that the person likes about you:

1.

2.

3.

If that person were talking to another about you, how would he or she describe you? Include the things in this description that the person values most about you.

How do you take care of this relationship? What do you do to nurture it and nourish it?

What does that significant person in your life do to nurture and nourish this relationship?

How is your life different because it has been touched by this person?

How did this relationship start?

Write a letter to this person and talk about this relationship. Include statements about the importance of the relationship for you and the impact this person has had on your life. Include specifics that show how the relationship has grown and "become," and what are your hopes and dreams with regard to the presence of this person in your life.

Chapter Twenty-one

PLAY —
AND THEN PLAY SOME MORE

W e've all heard the maxim: "All work and no play makes Jack a dull boy." Why is it that we put restrictions on play so that we have to earn it? We were told as children that we couldn't go out to play unless our homework was done. We had to eat our vegetables or there would be no dessert. All chores had to be done before we could go to the movies.

Is that how we learned that play comes second to responsibility? Is that how we have learned to be so serious rather than learning how to play for the sake of playing? Some believe that play is a waste of time. If "all work and no play makes Jack a dull boy," is dull what we want to be?

Dullness leads to boredom, and one then lacks spontaneity and energy. We cut off our creativity and become robots. We need to play more to be alive. In reality, we accomplish more work when we have time to play.

Action Today: Proclaim today Play Day. Even if you have to work, play at it. Find ways to enjoy your work.

Think kind thoughts of those you meet today and share funny thoughts or stories with them. Be free enough to let the kid inside of you come out and live. Remember, little kids get their hands and faces dirty, and know no boundaries. No dare is out of reach...no tree too tall...no puddle too wide.

Chapter Twenty-two

MAKE SOME MISTAKES

S omeplace along the line, we have been handed a bill of goods that is not healthy. We have grown up believing that we should be perfect, that we should never make mistakes, that we should always do everything right.

Those kinds of messages are pretty unhealthy because they take away creativity and wholeness: We lose spontaneity....we limit our own abilities....we discount any newness....we never can learn how to play or to relax or to enjoy ourselves. Our lives become so fixed on agendas and things we "have to do" that we learn never to develop a free spirit. We censor our creativity, and lose sight of joy and the moments of energy that are present in our day.

Until we learn to make mistakes and laugh at ourselves, we are prisoners — and our own jail-keepers. We have to stop being so hard on ourselves and begin to respect and like ourselves. I'm not just suggesting that we love ourselves but also that we LIKE ourselves. Liking ourselves implies that we know ourselves and take care of ourselves and learn to be gentle with ourselves.

It also implies that we are aware of the darker side of our personality and are in touch with things about us that have sharp edges and, at times, irritate people. No one is perfect. There are always things about all of us that we could work on and improve.

Learning to make mistakes is possible. We have to set out to learn the skill. It means being uncomfortable with ourselves for a while. It can feel awkward and stifling. But once we learn how to make mistakes, we stop being so hard on ourselves and on others, too.

Here is a homework assignment for the rest of your life: Make three mistakes a day on purpose. Anything over and above that earn bonus points, and you can score as many bonus points as you would like during each day. But you must make three mistakes a day on purpose.

What you will begin to do is breathe easier. You'll take a lot of pressure off your own shoulders. After a while, you'll begin to see that you are easier on others and not so quick to judge their actions or intentions. The pay-off is refreshing. You'll find you have more patience and are not as tense. You'll smile more (so the environment is now enriched).

Carry a little ruler in your head and picture it numbered from one to ten. Decide not to give every action of your life — or of the lives of those with whom you are interacting — a score of eight, nine or ten. Sometimes, the behavior only deserves a one, two or three. Reserve some of your energy for things that really need attention:

☐ Is a spilled glass of milk really deserving of an eight, nine or ten explosion?

☐ Do you really want to spend so much energy on a slammed door or a misplaced set of keys?

There is a wonderful principal that states: "Things worth doing are worth doing poorly." If we could only learn that instead of thinking that we have to do everything or the whole job. It is possible and healthy to just use whatever time we have available to us. But we were taught just the opposite and learned "the things worth doing are to be done perfectly and properly." Sometimes, we just don't have the time to do a total job, and we only raise our own frustration level if we wait until we have time to do the complete task:

We look out at our gardens and think we have to go out and pull out all the weeds. Why don't we just pull out the big ones?

When we are having company, we think we have to polish all the silverware. Why don't we just polish what we are going to use that evening?

When we think that way, tasks become accomplishable, and we take reaching perfection every time we move out of our expectations.

Mistakes teach us to relax. They teach us that perfection is not everything. We can learn a lot when we make a mistake. Sometimes, we even find out that there is another way of doing something that even ends up superior to the one solution we thought possible.

Think of a time something did not go the way you wanted it to go and you thought you had failed or made a mistake. Write about the situation.

What was the result of making a mistake?

Was it a crisis?

What did you learn about yourself because the situation did not work out the way you wanted it to?

What do you hear yourself say to yourself when you make a mistake?

Recall at least three situations where you were glad something didn't work the way you set out to make it work. Help yourself see some options and creative solutions:

1.

2.

3.

What is your reaction when you see others make mistakes? List two specific incidents:

1.

2.

Recall something you learned from a mistake and write how that resulted in a growth for you.

Chapter Twenty-three

PERCEPTIONS

s the glass half-empty or half-full?

It's up to you.

Do you want to make this day one of your good ones, or do you want to find things that are wrong and complain about everything?

It's up to you.

Listen to your thoughts and become aware of the fact you are either a positive or a negative person.

It's up to you:

• If everything bad happens to you and nothing ever goes the way you want it to go, then maybe you need a personality adjustment.

• If you keep on thinking those negative thoughts, you'll stop liking yourself. And you should know this: No one else will like you either.

• Set out to only be positive today. If you make a mistake — too bad. If you subtract your checkbook incorrectly — too bad. If someone doesn't like what you are doing — too bad. If you have two different socks on — too bad.

Action Today: This is a half-full day. Nothing is wrong; no one can upset me; and I can't do anything that I can't change tomorrow. I'll relax with myself and see only the positive in all that occurs.

It's up to me.

Chapter Twenty-four

LOOKING OUTWARD
INSTEAD OF INWARD

I t is a lot easier for us to see other people and decide what they are like than it is for us to look at ourselves and determine what we are like:

☐ We look at the way others act and make judgments on their character.

☐ We decide a lot about someone else by the choice of clothes he or she has made.

☐ We examine items like cars and boats and material possessions, and think they give us an insight into the world of somebody else.

☐ People's jobs and positions help us determine who they are.

☐ Parents often pass judgment on their children's friends, families and backgrounds with little to go on but outward appearances.

Information gathered in that way is rarely accurate. Many times, it is based on rumors; people spread false stories about others due to jealousy, rage, inaccurate information, personal choices, fears, selective listening and lack of perception. Those are only a few of the reasons we know only pieces and parts of other people's worlds and personalities.

Negative people have an odd trait of seeing only the wrongs of others. Others have faults and are improper. Negative people never look in the mirror to focus on the person reflected there; as a result, there is a missing link in that person's awareness.

Instead of figuring out others' values or whether the other is right or wrong, correct or incorrect, we should do a little personal inventory at times, and spend a bit of time on self-reflection and awareness. We should look ourselves squarely in the face to judge our own actions and behaviors.

There is a story about a very successful businessman who was dating a beautiful actress. The gentleman was growing fond of her and knew he was getting close to asking her to marry him. So he hired a private investigator to find out if there was anything in her past that might prevent a successful marriage. The businessman gave the detective no details other than her name.

The report came back that her background was flawless. There wasn't a single negative thing to report. Only one questionable factor surfaced: The actress was presently dating a businessman with a questionable character!

There is a lesson for us in that story. We need to see ourselves as well as seeing others. Seeing ourselves does not have to be navel gazing. The balance of looking out as well as looking in can be wholesome.

So often, our observations result in black/white

interpretations. We need to strive to see that gray may be a gift or a grace that allows us to relax more with what is in front of us. Instead of judging everything and everyone as black/white, it would be helpful if we could begin by putting just a polka dot or two in each picture.

We need to do this with ourselves, too. We need to re-learn some old things about ourselves, and to start to accept and respect ourselves.

Write the name of three family members and three friends:

NAME / BEHAVIOR / ACTION / BELIEF

Family 1:

Family 2:

Family 3:

Friend 1:

Friend 2:

Friend 3:

After each person you have listed, write a behavior or action or belief they hold with which you disagree.

Now write each name again:

NAME / POSITIVE / BELIEF

Family 1:

Family 2:

Family 3:

Friend 1:

Friend 2:

Friend 3:

After each person, write one positive thing about that person, or one belief they hold that you respect, or something you really like about them.

Re-read this positive list each day for a week and feel free to add more positive things to it.

Before two weeks pass, call each person and tell him or her what's on your positive list and thank them for being a presence (present) in your life.

Now write about YOU. List five positive qualities about yourself:

1.

2.

3.

4.

5.

Now list five things you want to change:

1.

2.

3.

4.

5.

Write two sentences about yourself that contain at least five positive adjectives that describe you:

1.

2.

Read those two sentences every day for a week.

Chapter Twenty-five

HOSPITALITY

T here is a beautiful quote in the Book of Hebrews that offers us an opportunity: "Do not neglect to show hospitality to strangers for by doing that some have entertained angels without knowing it."

Let us live that out today so that no one lacks our hospitality:

The way we greet another...

the smile we share...

the eye contact we keep...

the interest of the other that is conveyed by our body posture —

those are but a few gestures we can offer to show the warmth of our companionship to another. What you can learn about yourself as you listen differently to the stranger or stay open to her message can surprise you.

How sad to think we could have missed the opportunity to have an angel touch our heart and soul. How sad if we passed up that chance. What life-giving moments have escaped us!

Think what the world would be like if we treated

everyone with this message from Hebrews in mind. It would be awesome. We would lose our prejudices and make room for differences. We would truly hear the message of the sender and eliminate all misunderstandings in communication. We would have a warm feeling around our heart knowing something special has happened to us.

Action Today: Look at all the people you come in contact with as angels, and give them the dignity and respect each one deserves. Be touched by people who may not have yet realized they are angels and are negative and unhappy. They, too, carry angelic messages.

Chapter Twenty-Six

FREE YOUR SPIRIT

Maybe we should all rent a four-year-old for the weekend. That child would teach us perspective, wisdom and balance. We would learn that we need to wake up parts of us and become alive. We could truly learn how to live.

Many adults do not know how to use their heads, hearts, bodies and souls. We're always trying to separate pieces of who we are. Some of us never learned to see and hear and touch and taste and smell and dream and dance and laugh. Those people live by "shoulds" and "should-nots" and "always" and "never" and become (f)rigid people.

Age has nothing to do with it. You can become old as a very young child. Or you can chose to be a childlike old person. One is free and alive. The other has died. You don't have to be dead to die. There are a lot of people walking around who are not dead but have not yet learned how to live. They postpone and wait. It's never the right time. They never have what they need. Life is full of limitations and restrictions for such people. Unfortunately, they stop growing and decide to survive rather than to live.

Some people look for instant relief. Television tells us that pills do it quickly for us. There is an instant remedy for every ailment or pain. No need to suffer any inconvenience at all. So waiting and patience are not understood.

Laughter does not come easily in our world:

• People are confronted with disturbing news about the corruption that exists in the business world, sports arena and government agencies.

• We are aware of the crime rates in the United States and live in fear of being a statistic of the burglary, mugging, assault and robbery figures.

• We know that alcohol abuse accounts for thousands of homicides, domestic disputes and traffic fatalities.

• Child abuse and partner abuse statistics are astounding.

• Pregnancy rates are up for the teenage population.

• Nearly half of American's marriages end in divorce.

• Unemployment data are extremely high.

• It is estimated that more that 32 percent of Americans are poor.

So what is there to laugh about? Laughter is almost sacred. It's a spontaneous reflection that indicates freedom. Laughter discloses true joy, beauty and affirmation. It is the power to "see through" moments of humanness and despair. It is the ability to be free enough to know there is a balance and all can be well.

Some people wait for others to make them happy.

Some let others set the mood and attitude of their work area. Some let others determine the whens, hows, whys and ifs of their lives. For us to be whole and happy people, we need to own ourselves. All of us need to have a life!

If you're waiting for your friend or partner to go to a movie and she doesn't want to go, go alone or ask someone else to go with you. If you are waiting for a person to go to a concert and he doesn't want to go, find someone else. Our lives depend on our choices. We can spend a lot of time waiting for someone else to meet our needs — or we can find another way to have our needs met.

Life is worth living! It's important to live our life. Waiting for another person to decide to do things with us risks us never doing anything.

Write about a time when laughter broke the tension you were experiencing at a meeting or in a family interaction or at work.

What happened after the laughter started?

How have you used the skill in other situations?

Chapter Twenty-seven

ASK AND YOU RECEIVE

We must be careful what we ask for lest we get it.

I remember a woman who was dying of cancer telling me that once she had asked God for the blessing of good health until she saw all her children grown and settled. Her youngest had just married; a few days later, she was diagnosed with cancer.

What would happen if we instead asked for gifts like a day of laughter or a million joys, one following the other? Doesn't it sound exciting to be overdosed with happiness and to be able to blame the exhaustion we experience on laughing too much! Ah! What delight: to go to bed at night only able to identify the feeling of being happy all day.

Action Today: Ask your God for the gift of joy, laughter and humor. Then sit back and wait to live the experience. Look for the angels to carry those happy messages to you.

Maybe that's also the true meaning of "Ask and you shall receive." Oh, to believe! If the power of the request can be experienced in staying well until your children grow up, cannot the power also exist in positive experiences?

Chapter Twenty-eight

WISDOM IN OUR LIVES

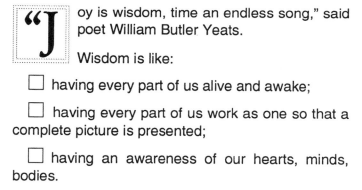

"**J**oy is wisdom, time an endless song," said poet William Butler Yeats.

Wisdom is like:

☐ having every part of us alive and awake;

☐ having every part of us work as one so that a complete picture is presented;

☐ having an awareness of our hearts, minds, bodies.

It's like coming alive. It's seeing, hearing, tasting, touching, feeling, perceiving and dreaming. It's being compassionate and caring and intelligent. It's being whole.

Most of the time, we do not allow ourselves the luxury of being so in touch with every moment that we feel the joy and wisdom that is present. To be a wise person is to be able to see beyond the moment in front of us and breathe into the next. It doesn't hold us captive and create un-freedom. Rather, it is a mind-blowing experience that takes us to creative awarenesses.

All of us who have ever had the privilege of knowing a wise old person (and it has nothing to do with chronological age) know what the experience is like. We sit in awe of their profound wisdom. It's not conveyed to us by a lot of words. The message comes through the person.

My little friend Amanda was dealing with the loss of her best friend, Barbara. They were inseparable, and their very presence always touched my heart. Amanda had gone blind a few months before Barbara died. Amanda didn't really understand this thing called death and was filled with questions about heaven, where Barbara was, spirits, where one's body goes and what happens then. She asked me a wonderful question one day in her search for some information.

"Anne, everyone is talking about Barbara being up there. Well, if she is up, what is down?"

That led us into a long, detailed conversation about heaven and hell, and what we both thought they were all about.

Amanda: "Well, what's the other place?"

Me: "What other place?"

Amanda: "You know — purr-ger-tory."

Me: "Oh, purgatory!" [I was aware I was speaking to an eight-year-old child. However, she had her questions lined up, and I was struggling to respond to her satisfaction.] "Well, some people believe that purgatory is a place that when a person dies and that person isn't ready to go to heaven, then that person would wait in purgatory until they are ready to go to heaven."

Amanda: "Oh, Anne, Barbara's not in purr-ger-tory. And we won't go to purr-ger-tory. We've all waited long enough."

Ah! The wisdom of an eight-year-old. She cut right through the words and applied the meaning to her truth. Amanda truly knew her friend. She knew of the waiting, the suffering and the long, weary, unexplained moments they had both lived. Yes, there was no need to wait any longer. Her friend had waited long enough, and her friend was in Heaven. How could anyone ever question that?

Wisdom has many faces. It knows no age, gender, educational level or religion. But once that wisdom touches you, you truly know joy. It expands your heart and changes your thoughts. YOU change.

Write about a person of wisdom who touched your life.

What was the message you heard through that person?

How has that message changed you?

What difference has come about for you because wisdom became joy?

Chapter Twenty-nine

PREJUDICES

J anuary 15 is the birthday of Dr. Martin Luther King. This courageous civil rights leader of the 1960s organized nonviolent marches that paved the way for demonstrations for equal rights and justice.

"We have learned to swim the sea like fishes and fly the sky like birds," he once wrote, "but we have not yet learned the art of living together as brothers."

Our vision gets limited; we get goal-oriented and find ourselves becoming violent with one another. Then that violence takes on the face of ignoring each other, or not listening to each other, or not caring.

Perhaps we are holding on to a prejudice. It may be about race, color, gender, sexual preference or nationality. It may be about children, animals, lawyers, bishops, co-workers. Ponder what would happen if we examined our prejudices and changed our minds.

Action Today: Get in touch with one of your prejudices. It won't take long before you will feel the prejudice, or see it, or hear yourself identify it. It may be the way people drive or shove to get ahead in line or just not seem to notice anyone else. Instead of being comfortable and maintaining the stereotype, change your opinion. Teach yourself there are other ways of looking at and judging others and their situations.

Chapter Thirty

OH JOY!

Here's what I know about joy:
- You cannot hold onto joy. It is not a possession you clutch in your hand. You can't grab it or capture it. You can't make a choice never to let go of it.

- It would be foolish to believe you can experience joy every single waking moment of our life.

- Joy truly comes when you are living and experiencing the present moment, and are in touch with that awareness. It implies being open and loving and aware of even yourself.

- Joy also implies that we have a sense of connection. We are not isolated people, and we cannot imprison ourselves.

- Joy is a way to know who we are to ourselves, who we are to others, and who others are to us.

- Joy expands our world to include all the goodness around us. We see beauty in flowers, in trees, in plants and animals, in stars and clouds, in works of art, in the faces of young children and in the old.

- Joy fills the emptiness of our lives and touches us with a reality of hope and life-energy. It's a shot in the arm. Joy is the push into the next moment of life that opens us to the grace of the moment.

• With joy in our lives, we know that nothing is really an accident. We begin to see all as a way to perceive things differently: We see mistakes as a way of learning a new way to do something....We perceive blocks in our path of life as stepping stones rather than stumbling blocks....We learn to view awkward moments as possibilities.

List two times in the last 24 hours when you were joyful:

  1.

  2.

Now write down how you can bring joy to someone else right now:

Go do what you wrote.

Chapter Thirty-one

PRESENCE

A n African proverb states: "Not to aid one in distress is to kill him in your heart."

How often we pass others without even realizing our ability to aid them. Aid comes in all shapes and sizes and colors and textures. We aid each other by our very presence. No presents are necessary. It is our presence that counts!

Even words are not always necessary. A gentle touch of the hand...an arm around a shoulder...an unexpected kindness...the gift of listening to a need...a nonjudgmental response...lending a hand to a project...finishing a task that has already been begun by another...sitting in a hospital room with a sick person — those are the things that keep us alive in each others' hearts. We create wonderful memories of those moments. They have a strange way of returning to us and filling our own hearts.

Action Today: Aid as many people as possible. Let us give life to each other and keep each other alive. Before you go to bed tonight, bring some of that energy you gave to others throughout the day back to your own being by recalling those life-giving moments you gave to others. Feel the connection between yourself and others.

Chapter Thirty-two

A NEW WAY OF LOOKING

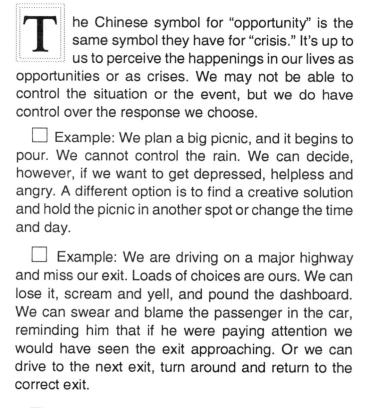

The Chinese symbol for "opportunity" is the same symbol they have for "crisis." It's up to us to perceive the happenings in our lives as opportunities or as crises. We may not be able to control the situation or the event, but we do have control over the response we choose.

☐ Example: We plan a big picnic, and it begins to pour. We cannot control the rain. We can decide, however, if we want to get depressed, helpless and angry. A different option is to find a creative solution and hold the picnic in another spot or change the time and day.

☐ Example: We are driving on a major highway and miss our exit. Loads of choices are ours. We can lose it, scream and yell, and pound the dashboard. We can swear and blame the passenger in the car, reminding him that if he were paying attention we would have seen the exit approaching. Or we can drive to the next exit, turn around and return to the correct exit.

The response to the situation or event is ours. The choice we make determines the outcome of the moment. So, if we don't like the outcome, all we have to do is to change our response. The situation or the event is what we tend to blame, but the power to make that choice is ours.

To be able to experience the joy and positive energy in the moment, it is important that we remember (or teach ourselves) that we can control our thoughts. We have 50,000 thoughts a day. We have to decide which ones we want to hold on to and let control our actions.

It is important to keep our self-talk positive and not buy into the negativity that can harm our psychological thought process. When we make a mistake or miss a turn, we may want to remind ourselves that it is not the end of the world and that nothing terrible is going to happen. Coincidences happen, and as Bernie Siegel reminds us: "Coincidences are God's way of staying anonymous."

How we could relax if we could believe that missing an exit, or buying the wrong brand of toilet paper, or forgetting a birthday, or making a mistake was just a "coincidence."

We may not be able to control what happens or the outcome of the situation but we can decide how we want to behave and act and think.

Recall three incidents that occurred in your life in the last two weeks. Write about them with as many details as you remember:

1.

2.

3.

Write your reactions and responses for each one
of these situations.

1.

2.

3.

For each, is there a way you could have seen the opportunity in the moment? (Find a way to do that.)

1.

2.

3.

Chapter Thirty-three

MY MOTHER'S BIRTHDAY

My mother's birthday is January 17. What a gift! Her life has been a blessing to so many. We need to celebrate life and the life-giving moments people like my Mom give to us.

These moments are filled with energy, joy and enthusiasm. They provide warmth, encouragement and support. These people are always there for us, loving us unconditionally. They embrace us with their arms and hearts, their smiles, and their very breath. We know the safety of their presence and the wisdom of their example. They awaken our souls. Truly, they are joy. Their lives are sacraments for us; they birth us into being and allow us to create who we are throughout our own life journey.

Action Today: Call someone who has touched you with the gift of life and tell her or him the blessing she or he is for you. You will massage that person with your message, and you will awaken the awareness of that person's giftedness in your own life. Then there will be two people who spend the day feeling warmth surrounding their hearts and wearing a smile that recalls the blessings we are to one another.

Chapter Thirty-four

CHECK YOUR ATTITUDES

T here is an old story about a man that came upon three masons working very hard at lifting up the heavy stones for the building they were constructing.

The man asked the first mason: "What are you doing?"

The mason looked up with anger and disgust, and replied, "What the hell does it look like? I'm working."

The man turned to the next mason and asked, "What are you doing?"

The second mason looked up, brushed the sweat from his brow, and replied, "I'm earning a living."

The man turned to the third mason and asked, "What are you doing?"

That mason looked up at the man with a glow in his eyes and replied, "I'm building a cathedral."

Which response fits your style?

☐ Are you the angry person who resents what is happening all around you and makes sure everyone knows it? Do you mutter comments under your breath or (even worse) loud enough for another to hear? Do you call everyone and anyone "jerk" or "idiot" or some other phrase that let's them know they are wrong and you, of course, are right?

Sometimes, that tells us more about the speaker than the one on whom the speaker passes judgment. Listen to yourself and see if you are a judgmental person who puts down others. Listen to your responses as people ask you what you do or what you are doing. If you are not happy or do not like yourself, you'll hear it in your response.

☐ Are you like the second mason, earning a living and doing his job? Is your life middle-of-the-road, and are you doing only what you need to do — nothing more and nothing less? You can be a robot and act like that, but there is no soul in that attitude.

☐ The third mason projected the balance, pride and focus that guarantee health and happiness. So often, the message is in the eyes! They glow and sparkle and generate energy. It is when the attitude is positive that one can be in touch with the reality of what is important to oneself.

You can own your choices and your actions, and see life as it is. When you have a purpose, your job, relationships and interests fall into perspective.

Which of the three masons describes you most of the time?

Write what you get in return for responding to situations that way. Be sure you list both positive and negative responses.

POSITIVE   **NEGATIVE**

List a person you know who always responds as the first mason:

...as the second mason:

...as the third mason:

What can you learn from these three people?

Chapter Thirty-five

FOCUS

L ittle children have not learned the art of blocking others with their judgments and negativity. They only know how to live this very moment and play. When that moment is over, they have forgotten it.

We should learn the art of playing from children and realize the endless energy present in their bodies. They could teach us how to create priorities and show us that everything is not work or responsibility. They would open our eyes to newness and life, the ability to laugh and giggle and trip and make mistakes, starting over and even looking at the same video several times. They possess the gift of attentiveness and the gift of ignoring something that is not important or does not hold their interest.

Little children are free enough to cuddle on our laps and persistent enough to nag us into doing what they would like to do. It is in the eyes of a child that we can see our God and are made aware of the awesomeness of life.

Action Today: Discover some of the wonderful childlike traits you have. Look at your own ability to play and laugh, to roll in the snow or to walk through a mud puddle. Remember that mistakes are not the things that define who we are. We have to learn from them and gain the wisdom of moving on. We can let go of our yesterdays...not yet live our tomorrows...and sap every living second of today.

Chapter Thirty-six

LIKING YOURSELF

There was a wonderful "Dennis the Menace" cartoon in the newspaper one day. He was climbing a tree with his faithful friend, Joey, close behind. Dawg was waiting on the ground under the tree, looking up at his owner. Dennis looked down to Joey on the limb below and said, "Always be proud of yourself, Joey. Sometimes, you're all you've got."

We can learn a lot from Dennis. Sometimes, we are all we've got. Yet many of us look to others for validation and affirmation. For many of us, self-esteem is defined by what others say to us or think of us. Some people can never believe they are good or even begin to believe in their own potential since they never look to themselves but only to others for this message. Sadly, there are those among us, who, even when they are told by others and credited for their accomplishments, still don't believe it.

Trusting ourselves is very difficult if we get into putting ourselves down and never believing in who we are. Maybe trusting ourselves comes from learning to be proud of ourselves like Dennis. Climbing a tree is an accomplishment. Learning to ride a bike, bake a pie, prepare a special meal, wallpaper a room, and even getting up in the morning on time are accomplishments. For one day, pat yourself on the back and live each deed you complete with pleasure.

What is one thing you have always wanted to learn to do, to make, to accomplish? Write about it.

What three blocks have prevented you from even beginning to learn this?

1.

2.

3.

Take each block and write one thing you can do to erase that barrier so you can begin to accomplish that dream of yours.

Block #1 can be erased by:

Block #2 can be erased by:

Block #3 can be erased by:

Now make a contract with yourself that you will set about beginning this by a certain date, but do not give yourself more than two weeks to begin. Be as specific as possible.

CONTRACT WITH MYSELF: I will

List also the resources you need to accomplish this; next to each resource, write what you need to be able to set about getting it.

RESOURCE: **NEEDS:**

Now, write the name of one person with whom you can share this goal and dream, and then ask this person to support you in this endeavor. Share the dates and resources needed with this person, and commit to report the outcome to this person. (Support is a wonderful thing!)

MY SUPPORTER:

Chapter Thirty-seven

REMEMBERING

All Soul's Day, November 2, is celebrated in many countries as a day for remembering the dead and a day for celebrating the presence of persons who touched our lives.

I was in Peru one year for this holiday and witnessed the reverence of this custom that each generation passes down to its children. There, everyone goes to the cemetery on All Saints Day, November 1 (also a national holiday in Peru) or on November 2, All Souls Day. The custom is to hold a picnic on the grave of a loved one, something which gives the feeling that death is really a festive occasion. The marketplace vendors cover their stalls with fresh flowers and artificial arrangements, and people purchase them to place on the graves of their deceased.

The whole family is part of this ritual. The trip to the cemetery is an all-day venture. Family members carry with them the flowers to decorate the grave and food so they may sit for hours upon arriving at the grave, talking with one another about the person who has died. It is customary for songs to be sung, and for people to share stories about the deceased and remember the dead with respect.

All of this passes the history of that person on to

the younger members of the family and teaches them to honor those who have gone before them. The food is usually the favorite food of the deceased. They also bring breads ornately decorated in the shapes of animals and share them with others in the cemetery. I was given a llama and a bird, and told this tradition was similar to our sharing valentines in the United States.

How healthy for us to remember our connections with those who have touched our lives and helped us know who we are. How healthy to remember we carry these people in our thoughts and in our hearts and to respect them with the sharing of these memories.

Action Today: Remember those people who have touched your life and helped you know who you are. Remember especially those who have died and who live on in your memory. Take out a picture of that person, visit the cemetery, or call someone who knew that person and share some stories together so that you feel connected to that person. You may even want to prepare the favorite meal or enjoy the favorite beverage of that person so that memory can warm your heart, too. As Sister James M. Barrie says, "God gave us our memories so we might have roses in December."

Chapter Thirty-eight

JUDGMENTS

uman beings are quick to make judgments about other people, events, actions and even the lack of behaviors:

• We judge others' motives and reasons.

• We put people into categories and isolate them with labels.

• We decide whether we like people based on what they do, how they talk, their backgrounds, the level of their education, how they dress, and other equally superficial qualities.

What would happen if we stood in front of someone who looked very different from us (perhaps someone who frightened us) and instead of judging him, just stood there?

What if we stood with a stance of openness and wonder?

What if we stood with a sense of awe and surprise?

What if our agenda was to learn something instead of a preconceived knowing something?

What would happen then?

"Raisin in the Sun" is a wonderful play about a

black family struggling to survive not only in the world with its economic and social pressures but also within the family system itself. The grandmother, the matriarch of the family, offers some wise words to her daughter as she reprimands her for judging and belittling her brother.

The scene takes place after the son has made a decision regarding the family money that had been saved to buy a longed-dreamed-of house. The motives of the son were good, but the outcome was devastating to the family. His sister, in touch only with the loss, lashes out at her brother, yelling and screaming about how much she hates him.

The grandmother chastises her daughter and powerfully reminds her: "There is always something left to love, and if you ain't learned that, you ain't learned nothing....Child, when do you think is the time to love somebody the most, when they done good and made things easy for everybody? Well, then, you ain't learning — because that ain't the time at all. It's when he's at his lowest and can't believe in himself 'cause the world done whipped him so. When you starts measuring somebody, measure him right, child, measure him right. Make sure you done taken into account what hills and valleys he come through before he got to wherever he is...."

Those are powerful words, words we may want to hold in our hearts the next time someone disappoints us or chooses to act in a way we disapprove.

And we don't have to apply those thoughts solely to those we love and are comfortable with. We can apply them to politicians, bishops, next-door neighbors and people of different faiths. We can remember them while watching the six o'clock news and while reading the newspaper. We can recall them while waiting in line at the supermarket and finding our patience wearing thin because we have chosen the "wrong line" with people ahead of us questioning prices, using food stamps or taking time buying lottery tickets.

I work a lot with adolescents; they are my favorite group of people. They are real. They have not permanently put on their "faces:" the adult masks we have learned to wear. Adolescents tell it like it is.

Adolescence is a stage of searching for selfhood. "Who am I?" is the question they are struggling to answer. As a result, they often try on different behaviors in an attempt to answer the question. They imitate others' actions, dress like others and find a language others understand to communicate this awkward stage. Adults have a hard time understanding some of their choices. It's even harder when the child is OURS!

A few years back, there was a terrific kid named Alex. He was 13 and the son of a woman who had adopted him from El Salvador when he was three. She was a dedicated single parent who loved her son more than life itself. Alex's best friend, Jason, had committed suicide in January, and Alex was obsessed with this act. He talked only of killing himself so he could be with Jason.

Alex's mother asked me if he could come to the adolescent group that I hold each week at our counseling center. I faintly knew him because we all belonged to the same parish, and I would often see him serve Sunday Mass. I also knew that Alex was a hyperactive child and under the care of both a psychiatrist and a psychologist. My reaction to his mother was that this group would certainly be an overload for him. She replied that he would not speak to the other two doctors, and this was her attempt to have him talk. I finally agreed to see him.

When she brought him in for the initial session, he was very nervous and maintained no eye contact with me. The session was supposed to be an information gathering session, but it was not much more than an exchange between his mother and me. At the end of the session, I asked Alex if he would agree to attend two meetings of the group; then, if he didn't like it, he needed to share that with me and we would look for alternatives. Alex agreed.

Throughout his first session, he never looked up from the floor. When asked to respond to something, he would shake his head seven times before he answered verbally.

Alex returned the second week. This time, he looked at the floor, up at someone, then back at the floor, and back up again. His verbal response to questions came after only three shakes of his head.

Alex came back for the third session. Now I was feeling we were really making progress. This time, Alex looked around the room at the group members. I jumped at this and said, "Alex, it must be terrible to lose your best friend. Do you want to talk about Jason?"

Alex said, "No, I'm not ready yet."

Believing we must respect each other's space and time, I asked him if he would do an exercise with the group. I asked if he would look at each member as they offered one positive thing about him. His only response could be, "Thank you very much." He agreed.

The group members never let me down. They all looked at Alex and said wonderful things to him about his sensitivity and ability to care so deeply. After each comment, Alex said, "Thank you very much."

That was a Tuesday. Alex hanged himself on Thursday.

At the funeral Mass, his mother addressed those in attendance. She told us of her gratitude for the roles we had played in his life. Then she told stories about him. Alex was always "doing things" in school, and it was not uncommon for her to receive several phone calls regarding his behavior. She admitted the calls came with such frequency that they were no longer any cause for anxiety or panic. Then she told one of these stories that helped me know of the depth of Alex.

One day, the teacher called to tell her that Alex had a communion wafer in his pocket. Waiting for him to come home from school, Alex's mom worked herself into a fever pitch. As he walked through the door, she screeched, "Alex, they called from school and said you have a host in your pocket. Do you?"

Alex readily admitted he did.

"Why do you have a host in your pocket?"

He replied: "I don't have anything else to give you for your birthday, Mom."

Alex knew what was important to his mother. We all learned a bit about the spirituality of a 13-year-old loving son, our friend Alex.

We judge. We don't know each other's stories. No one truly knows what goes on in another's world, but our judgments can create another wall that blocks us from seeing the other for who he or she is.

List three people about whom you have made a judgment. (These can be political figures, family members, etc.):

1.

2.

3.

Write the judgment regarding each:

1.

2.

3.

Now write one thing you can do to open yourself to see or hear another point of view regarding each of these.

1.

2.

3.

You might want to repeat this a month from now to see if you have changed.

Chapter Thirty-nine

SURROUND YOURSELF WITH LAUGHTER

P eople who help us laugh are truly gifts to us:

☐ They give us energy and help us stay balanced.

☐ They help us keep things in perspective and remind us we do not have to be perfect.

☐ They teach us acceptance of self and others.

☐ They empower us with the hope and belief that negativity can rob us of. Discouragement diminishes. Depression lifts. Smiles appear. Risks are taken.

I read of the tragic accident that paralyzed actor Christopher Reeve. Here was a strong, strikingly muscular, active man. An expert horsemen, he was nevertheless thrown from his mount and is now in a wheelchair, paralyzed from the neck down.

After the initial ordeal, he told of a friend's visit that changed his attitude and gave him life. Reeve was extremely depressed when comedian Robin Williams appeared in his hospital room dressed outlandishly as a Russian doctor. Reeve admitted that this was the first time he had laughed since the accident. He added that it was at that moment he knew he was going to be all right. The gifts of friendship, caring and laughter gave him hope and inspired him.

When we laugh, we keep our hopes alive. We empower ourselves and believe that change can happen, that things can get better, that at least, we do not have to opt for hopelessness. Laughter does not erase pain; it gives us the ability to handle pain.

Sorrow, pain, suffering and loss are all part of life. In Proverbs 14:13, we read, "Even in laughter, the heart is sorrowful." Sometimes, we have a mistaken notion that laughter implies everything is wonderful and perfect, but laughter is more like putting on a pair of sunglasses. They don't cancel the sun; they just allow people to be more comfortable and relax their eyes so they can see more clearly.

It is important that we put in our lives people who can be sunglasses for us and people who possess the same gifts Robin Williams has. These gifts are in all of our lives. Some of us are not aware of them and immediately claim we do not know anyone who can tickle our hearts with joy. In reality, they are there; and when we open ourselves to that awareness, we begin to see we have lots of these gifts in our lives.

Action Today: Be aware of the people who touch your heart and soul with the gift of a smile or the twinkle in their eyes that carries the energy of joy. Stay in touch with your own feelings of peace and contentment in their presence. Laugh more today than yesterday.

Chapter Forty

LIVE LONGER

E vidence suggests that optimists live longer than pessimists. It has been proven that optimists catch fewer infectious diseases than pessimists. Optimists have better health habits than pessimists. Even our immune system works better when we are optimistic.

We need to work on changing messages that create pessimistic attitudes. If we put ourselves down when we fail or think of ourselves as not good, we create negative thinking patterns that do us in. We learn how to be victims — and then we become helpless.

We have become a people who like to feel bad. People greet each other with an itemized list of how they feel: "I have such a headache"..."My head is killing me"..."I can't eat a thing..."My stomach is so bad"..."My back is breaking." It's no wonder that Valium and Tagamet are the most widely sold drugs in the country. It has been documented that 75 percent of daily conversation is negative. Some people wake up in the morning and start the day complaining about getting up. Then the weather outside is never right. It's either too hot or too cold; it's raining or snowing. Immediately, these people begin thinking of things that they have to do. They begin dreading the trip to the grocery store. Of course, they will get into the line that moves the slowest and the one where the person in front of them uses a million coupons to save $2.

They fill their day with "have to's." There is no fun, no free time, no enjoyment. There are just things that must be done. No wonder such folks are exhausted a few minutes after they get up in the morning!

Here's a prescription you can fill yourself:

- We have to teach ourselves to enjoy life again.

- We need to slow down long enough to be able to have a conversation with somebody else.

- We must smile more. Research has proven that how you look affects the way you feel. Even pretending to be happy gets you to feel happy.

- We need to spend time eating with people, and talking and listening to each other.

But we have become a culture of convenience, so we rush every place. We have cellular telephones so we never have to wait or find a phone. We use our microwave ovens so our dinners will be ready in three minutes so we can swallow them in two minutes. We have lost the art of enjoying food. Instead of sitting at our kitchen tables and sharing the stories of our day, we eat on the run. We have become more interested in the fat content of our food than in the nourishment that food provides the body, soul and mind.

To live longer, we must live one minute at a time — truly live each. For some, that may mean living one second at a time. We've heard the beautiful quote:

"Yesterday's the past, tomorrow's the future, but today is a gift. That's why it's called the present."

What were the first thoughts you had this morning when you got up? Write as many as you remember:

Do you need to start your day over? You can if you want to. Begin it again right now. Put a big smile on your face. Force it if you have to. Now tell yourself how wonderful the day is going to be. Write out the new message you are giving yourself:

Message to myself:

List two or three people who are pessimists. Write
how you feel when you are in their presence:

PERSON   FEELING
1.

2.

3.

List two or three people who are optimists. Write
how you feel when you are in their presence:

PERSON   FEELING
1.

2.

3.

It's your choice. You are the only one who can
make you happy. Write out your choice:

My choice:

Chapter Forty-one

WAYS TO COMMUNICATE

S ometimes, we have to find creative ways to reach out to each other. Words are always there. Still, distance sometimes creates barriers, and sometimes misunderstandings do not heal.

We communicate with words, letters, cards, gifts, smiles, eye contact, hugs through other persons and the use of symbols.

From 1558 to 1829, the Roman Catholic Church in England was forbidden to openly practice its faith. Yet its members developed ways to communicate the gift of faith in a coded song known as "The Twelve Days of Christmas."

The 12 days were from December 25 (Christmas) to January 6 (Epiphany). The "true love" referred to God. The repetition of the melody signified God's continual renewal of His gifts:

1. A partridge is a symbol of Christ. The partridge will feign injury to protect nestlings who are defenseless, just as defenseless as we are before Satan without Christ. A pear tree is the symbol of the salvation, just as the apple tree signifies the downfall.

2. Two turtle doves symbolizes the Old Testament sacrifice offered by even the poorest of people.

3. Three French hens, valued for their beauty and rarity, symbolize the gifts of the Three Wise Men and the theological virtues of faith, hope and love.

4. Four calling birds represent the four major prophets and the four evangelists, the former announcing Christ's coming and the latter proclaiming His message.

5. Five golden rings connote the perfect circle of Faith: God's love for us, our love for God and our love for one another. The number five refers to the five obligatory sacraments and the five books of the Old Testament in the Pentateuch.

6. Six geese a-laying represent the six days of creation.

7. Seven swans a-swimming are the seven gifts of the Holy Spirit and the seven works of mercy. The number seven is the number of completion in the Bible.

8. Eight maids a-milking are the eight beatitudes as well as the eight times during the year that were prescribed at that time for the reception of the Eucharist.

9. Nine ladies dancing are the nine ranks of angel choirs and the nine fruits of the Holy Spirit.

10. Ten lords a-leaping are the 10 commandments.

11. Eleven pipers are the eleven apostles proclaiming the Resurrection of Jesus.

12. Twelve drummers are the twelve minor prophets of the Old Testament and the twelve points of the Apostles Creed. While also referring to the twelve

tribes of Israel and the Apostles, twelve represents completion and fullness.

You see, there are always ways to communicate our thoughts, feelings and values. If a whole church can find a way to communicate with its members, we need to find ways to be connected to people in our life. Words are only symbols. The importance is the connection we have with another. That is what energizes us and bonds us. Without this, we shrivel and can die.

Action Today: Find a way to make a connection with someone. Find the "right" card or write a poem or song. If the Roman Catholic Church in England could create a song that communicated the gift of faith, you can create something to communicate your gift to another. Be sure you don't let the evening pass before you connect. Be as creative as you can and as symbolic as possible.

Chapter Forty-two

HUGS

Touching is probably one of the most important gifts we give to each other. If a baby is not held, it dies. We never lose the need to have someone put her arm around us or take hold of our hand. We all need the human touch; otherwise, we shrivel up and die.

But isn't it strange that the thing we all need so much is so often the one thing that we are afraid of?

I received a piece of mail that contained only a quote about hugging. The author was unknown. But the words were powerful:

HUGGING

Hugging is healthy

- It helps the body's immune system which keeps you healthier.

- It cures depression, reduces stress and induces sleep.

- It is invigorating, rejuvenating, and it has no unpleasant side-effects.

- Hugging is nothing less than a miracle drug.

• Hugging is practically perfect: There are no moving parts, no batteries to wear out, no periodic checkups. It is low-energy consumption, high-energy yield, inflation-proof, non-fattening, with no monthly payments, no insurance requirements, theft-proof, non-taxable, non-polluting and, of course, fully returnable!

What more can be said? It feels good to get a hug. It communicates volumes. Wouldn't if be wonderful if we made a vow to hug ten times a day? I'll bet there would be a lot more smiles around. Little kids don't seem to have a problem getting their quota of hugs. How about you?

What do hugs mean to you?

Are you more comfortable with some hugs? If so, why?

Do you remember a time that you really needed a hug and someone was there for you? Write about it.

Is there someone you would like to reach out to and hug? Who? What are the risks for you?

Can you ask for a hug when you need one?

Don't let the day go by without at least three hugs.

Chapter Forty-three

SUCCESS

We place too much emphasis on succeeding. We use success to measure who we are and what our worth is and how much we are liked and respected. We "measure" ourselves by how much we get done. How sad!

Did you ever look at a parent eyeing a report card? The first thing they look at and comment on is the marks. How high are they? Why aren't they higher?

Employers judge their employees on how much gets accomplished and produced. Often, words of praise are not heard, but hardly a flaw goes by unannounced.

We even judge God on how much gets accomplished and how many prayers are answered and how things are going the way we want them to go.

Confucius stated: "In all things, success depends on previous preparation; and without such preparation, there is sure to be failure." I guess that means that we have to work towards the success and that we need to be responsible all along the journey toward accomplishment. We need not judge ourselves along the way since we are walking toward the accomplishment. Each step will define the story. Each word of the story is written by us.

It is important to be aware of our own successes. We all need a pat on the back, and sometimes we have to pat ourselves. This is true humility. When we are free enough to acknowledge our accomplishments and successes, we are humble. We are also being responsible since these gifts and accomplishments are a part of us.

Action Today: Recall at least two successes that you have accomplished. Tell at least two people about them. Call someone up today and acknowledge a success of theirs. Praise them for that success.

Chapter Forty-four

LOVE BENEFITS

"**L**ove" is a strange word. We use it in regards to everything. We love people and animals and food and flowers. Everyone is looking and searching for love. Love makes people act differently. Sometimes, love even causes tears. Love eases burdens. Love feels good. Love songs are written so this strange feeling can be expressed with soft sounds of music emphasizing the words.

We hear that "love makes the world go 'round" and "love means you never have to say you're sorry." When lovers are together, they find reasons not to leave each other. Gifts are purchased to say "I love you."

Now we are finding out that true love (is there any other?) can aid the immune system. It promotes healing and extends one's life span. Longevity magazine reported the phenomenon of true love being beneficial to both the lover and the one loved: "One key to love's medicinal power may be the 'lover's high,' the euphoric state produced when amphetamine-like substances called phenythethylamines are released in the brain during the excitment phase of falling in love."

It also reported that a 1992 Ohio State University

College of Medicine study found couples who acted less loving toward each other had decreased levels of disease-fighting antibodies and T-cells. A decrease of antibodies and T-cells causes illness and helplessness — and even death.

Recently, Life magazine reported about twin girls, Kyrie and Brielle Jackson, who had been born 12 weeks early. They immediately were placed in separate incubators. Kyrie, who weighed two pounds, three ounces, slept very peacefully. Brielle, the smaller twin, had breathing and heart-rate problems. She did not gain any weight and fussed when anyone tried to comfort her.

Then a nurse tried a technique called "double bedding" and put the sisters together for the first time since they shared a womb. Brielle snuggled up to Kyrie and calmed right down. With her sister near, Brielle began to thrive.

Ah! The power of touch.

Why are we so afraid of loving and trusting? We build walls around our hearts and protect ourselves from the very passion we are yearning for. We choose to die instead of living with the strength that the power of physical touch gives to us.

Write a love letter to a significant person in your life. Be sure to write the words "I love you."

Re-read the letter. Now write how YOU feel. How does your body feel and your heart feel?

My body feels:

My heart feels:

Write about a time someone told you that they loved you. Write how you felt and how those words sounded to you.

Recall a special dinner or trip or party that you experienced with someone you love. Write about what happened and about the feelings you have because of the presence of that special person.

Recall when someone reached out to you and touched your hand or gave you a hug. What message was really given?

AFTERWORD

It has been wonderful sharing these stories with you. My hope is that they have helped you like the person you see in the mirror a bit more. That person is so special. You must take care of that person and respect yourself enough to grow a bit more everyday. We owe it to ourselves to cherish this gift of self.

Tell your own stories. Listen to others' stories. "POLISH YOUR SOUL AND SPRUCE UP YOUR HEART" with these stories. The Hawaiian people have a wonderful phrase they use as a greeting when they meet someone they haven't seen in a long time. They immediately say, "Let's talk story!" When you start telling your stories, listen with your heart to the messages and meanings. Value those memories and messages. They are pieces of you. Treat them with respect. These stories have created the person you look at in the mirror.

And share your stories with others. As we share our stories, we are connected with others, and our hearts and souls are lighter because of the joy that connects us.

Happy story-telling!

Books by Canticle Press
Mail Order Form

Two Children Who Knew Jesus $6.95
by Eileen Lomasney, CSJ
Light From Another Room $10.00
by Eileen Lomasney, CSJ
Jiggle Your Heart and Tickle Your Soul $10.00
(The Uses of Joy and Laughter in Attaining Health and Happiness)
by Anne Bryan Smollin, CSJ
Polish Your Soul and Spruce Up Your Heart $10.00
(How to Like What You See in the Mirror)
by Anne Bryan Smollin, CSJ
The Singing Bird Will Come: An AIDS Journal $10.95
by John R. Noonan, Ph.D., edited by Mary Rose Noonan, CSJ

Please send the following books:

_____

_____

_____

Name: _____

Address: _____

City: _____State:_____Zip:_____

Phone: _____

Shipping: Please add **$4.00** to your order for shipping and handling of 1-3 books, **$5.00** for 4-6 books, **$6.00** for 7-10 books. For bulk-order discounts, call (518) 783-3604.
Sales Tax: Please add sales tax for books shipped to NYS residences or supply tax-exempt number. New York State law requires **8%** sales tax on shipping and handling as well as on merchandise.

Please make checks payable to **Canticle Press, Inc.** and mail to:
Canticle Press, Inc.
385 Watervliet-Shaker Road
Latham, New York 12110-4799

Books by Canticle Press
Mail Order Form

Two Children Who Knew Jesus $6.95
by Eileen Lomasney, CSJ
Light From Another Room $10.00
by Eileen Lomasney, CSJ
Jiggle Your Heart and Tickle Your Soul $10.00
(The Uses of Joy and Laughter in Attaining Health and Happiness)
by Anne Bryan Smollin, CSJ
Polish Your Soul and Spruce Up Your Heart $10.00
(How to Like What You See in the Mirror)
by Anne Bryan Smollin, CSJ
The Singing Bird Will Come: An AIDS Journal $10.95
by John R. Noonan, Ph.D., edited by Mary Rose Noonan, CSJ

Please send the following books:

_____

_____

_____

Name: _____

Address: _____

City: _____State:_____Zip:_____

Phone: _____

<u>Shipping</u>:   Please add **$4.00** to your order for shipping and handling of 1-3 books, **$5.00** for 4-6 books, **$6.00** for 7-10 books. For bulk-order discounts, call (518) 783-3604.

<u>Sales Tax</u>:   Please add sales tax for books shipped to NYS residences or supply tax-exempt number. New York State law requires **8%** sales tax on shipping and handling as well as on merchandise.

Please make checks payable to **Canticle Press, Inc.** and mail to:
Canticle Press, Inc.
385 Watervliet-Shaker Road
Latham, New York 12110-4799